"There are two completely different worlds of marketing right now and each thinks the other is wrong, but one is stealing so much business from the other one."

– Kevin Simonson

"During an audit, a potential client literally slapped their forehead on the other end of the line. We took a look at their Adwords account and discovered that a huge percentage of their spend was going to keywords for the most low revenue, low margin item in their catalog, and performance was horrible. Their previous agency barely worked on account over the last 3 months."

....

"Earlier this year I had coffee with a consultant who audited the programmatic advertising for a major corporation here in New York and found something that should have shocked us, but didn't. His client budget was over $30 million for programmatic for the year across 21 brands, all of of which are female-focused products. While auditing programmatic for one of those products, he found that $100,000 of a $200,000 test served ads on Grindr, a gay men's dating app."

....

"A large consumer brand fired their marketing agency and hired employees in-house to run the campaigns instead. Our agency came in as advisors to help build their team and offer industry-specific insight they couldn't get on their own. Once we arrived, we found out that the brand had been paying over $100,000 a month in fees, for around $1 million in media spend, while results were terrible."

"Uber filed a $40 million lawsuit against Fetch Media, a mobile ad agency. The ride sharing company claimed the firm improperly billed them for fake online ads and took credit for app downloads it had nothing to do with. Around the same time, Fetch's global head of media, Steve Hobbs, told Adweek that a significant number of downloads in Fetch's system are flagged as suspicious, saying that, where there's money, there is fraud."

"An old client of ours from a media company transitioned to another organization. He sat down with his external marketing agency to review. Within minutes of chatting, he began seeing every red flag in the book. Inappropriate contract length, insane guarantees, cold and impersonal autopilot technologies that provided low client service, and so on. The agency even said that paying for Google Ads improves organic Google results! (It doesn't.) Our old client knew he was being taken for a ride, so he fired the agency and brought us in immediately."

"One of our competitors, another "performance" marketing agency, was brought in to replace us by the CEO of a major corporation to do user acquisition on Facebook and Instagram, to the chagrin of the client's head of marketing. Within weeks of starting their engagement, they did such a terrible job, losing massive sums of revenue, that internal employees started sending me messages about how bad our competitor was doing. Less than two months later, they fired our competitor and we received an agreement to take over their accounts, turning around performance."

"We were attending a digital marketing conference. An executive with a big alcohol client was telling this story about how he blew through $6 million in a month of his client's digital budget. And the report that was handed to the client at the end of the project said that their budget was executed in full and on time. Meanwhile, the executive was just laughing his head off about how much money he made off of that personally."

....

"A recruiting company spent $35k over a 2-month period on their jobs campaign with no conversion tracking. Including extremely generic keywords like 'part-time. This is known as cookie stuffing, meaning, taking credit for purchases that can't be attributed to your campaign."

....

"Criteo, a popular retargeting company that focuses on programmatic display advertising, had an undisclosed relationship with a notorious adware company. According to an article on Seeking Alpha, they were sued for regularly injecting adware into users' personal computers and placing ad inventory on numerous shady websites with suspicious traffic, to drive up revenue attribution figures."

....

"We were attending a retail expo. And we kid you not, an executive from a Big Five agency (Publicis, Interpublic, Omnicom, WPP, Dentsu-Aegis) told us: "I spend a third of my time delivering value for my clients, I spend a third of my time selling them shit they don't need, and the other third of my time is profit."

WHY WE WROTE THIS BOOK

We feel a moral obligation to make a dent in the advertising universe.

We wrote this book not only to shine a light on what's happening and why it's wrong, but importantly, to help educate all parties involved:

CEOs, CMOs, CFOs, brands of all sizes, marketing agencies, ad tech companies, private equity and venture capital firms, consultants, customers, and anyone else who is part of the digital marketing ecosystem.

Whichever one of those words most describes your role in the digital marketing world, we're here to help. We want to fix this mess. Because we're not doomsday sayers. We may be skeptical, but we're not cynical.

If you're like us, if you have even the smallest desire to create greater clarity and trust; to establish higher standards of accountability for digital brands; to promote transparent business practices in the digital marketing world: you've come to the right place.

Copyright © 2018 by Kevin Simonson,
John Pellinghelli & Ryan Markman

Edited by Regan Colestock
Creative Direction by Scott Ginsberg
Cover Art & Layout by Jeff Braun of Trifecta Creative

All rights reserved. This book or any portion thereof may not be reproduced or used in any manner whatsoever without the express written permission of the publisher except for the use of brief quotations in a book review.

Printed in the United States of America

Metric Digital, LLC
394 Broadway 5F
New York, NY 10013

www.metricdigital.com

Ordering Information:
Quantity sales. Special discounts are available on quantity purchases by corporations, associations, and others.
For details, contact the publisher at the address above.

AD FRAUD, INCOMPETENCE AND EVERYTHING IN BETWEEN

But how did we end up here?

Where did the advertising world go wrong?

And how is it possible that many of the clients we work with have already worked with 3+ agencies in the last few years before working with us?

Something is broken in the digital marketing world.

Restricted client account access. Unethical spending. Broken tracking. Incorrect ad placement.
Ignorant service providers. Unethical guarantees.
Embarrassing client service. Billions of dollars wasted.
Contracts where incentives are not aligned.

We're seeing toxic agency-client relationships in which unethical, unprofessional and unacceptable business practices end up wasting millions of company dollars and driving marketing departments crazy.

And the worst part is, a lot of executives at marketing agencies, ad tech software businesses, and even media companies know about and perpetuate this trend. Most are not incentivized to fix it.

That's why we've coined a term for it: *badvertising*.

Badvertising (n, bad-ver-tahy-zing):
a state of toxic agency-client or publisher-client relationships, characterized by a lack of transparency and by unethical or unprofessional business practices.

See also: how big agencies are screwing big companies out of big money.

We aim to help you understand what badvertising is, where it came from, how it affects your daily work, and what steps you can take to protect yourself (and your brand) from being a victim of it in the future.

TABLE OF CONTENTS

INTRODUCTION
- What are the different types of badvertising?
- Who are we, and why should you listen to us?

PART 1: HISTORICAL CONTEXT
- What caused the trend of toxic agency-client relationships?
- Who is most affected by badvertising?

PART 2: CURRENT LANDSCAPE
- Have you been badvertised?
- Where is digital marketing today?

PART 3: STRATEGY & TACTICS
- What are the questions you should be asking your Facebook Marketing Agency?
- What are the questions you should be asking your SEM Agency?
- What are the questions you should be asking your Email Marketing Agency?
- Is your agency helping grow your business, or just making your ads?

- Is programmatic advertising the right path for your brand?
- Is your agency ethically outsourcing, or intentionally misleading?
- Is your agency opening the digital books and building trust?
- What's the case for transparency from the agency's perspective?

PART 4: THE FUTURE

- Where will marketing go next?

APPENDIX

- Preparing Your Brand for Growth
- About the Authors

WHAT ARE THE DIFFERENT TYPES OF BADVERTISING?

Based on our experience, we'll be breaking it down into a few categories:

AD FRAUD

- Perpetrated by agencies that are trying to cover their ass for some bad work they know they are doing

- Perpetrated by ad tech platforms in the programmatic display world that purposefully do not have transparent systems to allow clients to see how dollars are being spent, because they are making money off of fraudulent spend.

- Locking clients out of ad accounts, obscuring billing, and charging an invisible fee that is intentionally hidden from the client

EXAMPLE: An ad tech company reports more impressions and more ad spend than was actually delivered, and the company keeps the difference.

BAD WORK

- Marketers running campaigns that they have no business running.

- Hiring the wrong people for the job, i.e. juniors executing senior level work
- Big agencies selling services they don't know how to fill, which ends up wasting a ton of client time money.
- Faking it until they make it, except they never actually make it

EXAMPLE: An agency that you have contracted for design and development work offers to manage your Facebook Advertising, despite the fact that they have no experience. They end up wasting your ad spend.

Now, it's okay if this has happened to you. It's not your fault, and you're not alone. We want to equip you with the tools to prevent badvertising from happening in the future.

Look, we understand that you're placing your trust in your marketing agency doing a good job, because they said they would. But you also don't have time to micromanage your agency. You should be able to trust them to do a good job.

In fact, here's proof that you're not alone, and that badvertising has reached critical mass:

The Association of National Advertisers, in their annual study about the state of programmatic media buying, listed many of the concerns around transparency and ad fraud that brands have been increasingly experiencing.

According to their research, a large majority (78%) of respondents are either concerned or very concerned about brand safety issues. Only 40% of respondents are comfortable or very comfortable about the transparency they receive with their media investments. And one third are uncomfortable or very uncomfortable, citing factors including hidden costs, too many middlemen, and uncertainty on where ads actually run.

One brand who participated in the study said it best:

"There are too many middlemen and layers between inventory source and buyer, including agency services that provide an unclear picture of what our working media actually is."

Plus, in response to that widely publicized study, Gideon Spanier wrote in Campaign Live about how the Federal Bureau of Investigation was actually looking into media trading and transparency in the US advertising market.

According to the release, they're investigating corporate fraud, aka white-collar crime, including illicit transactions designed to evade regulatory oversight and kickbacks. Not surprisingly, all of the agencies denied wrongdoing.

We hear, read, and discuss stories like this on a daily basis. Peers in the industry even complain, yeah, we know, digital marketing is messed up. Even the ones who are the worst offenders.

And we know this is a real thing. We've been in this business for over a decade or have been buying Facebook ads essentially since you have been able to buy them. Frankly, we're sick of it. And we don't want badvertising to happen to you. Or, if it has already happened to you, we want to help you take back control.

WHO ARE WE AND WHY SHOULD YOU LISTEN TO US?

Before we go any further, a quick origin story about your authors.

In 2013, Kevin Simonson was working as the Director of Media Operations for a Facebook Ad Tech Startup buying Facebook ads. He ran Facebook performance marketing for clients at an ad tech firm that went bankrupt after the CEO was naked on the front page of Gawker. This is (unfortunately) not a joke and very close to an episode of Silicon Valley.

This was back when Facebook was brand new for marketers and you just had to figure it out. In the end, the tech didn't take them as far as hoped and the company disbanded. But Kevin was able to figure out how to drive revenue for brands through Facebook in the process. When he informed his clients that the company was over, every single one of them offered him a job.

Kevin was very close to going to work with one of his favorite clients ever, NatureBox, but decided he didn't want to move to the west coast. Instead, he kept a couple clients on as a freelancer while he went to learn about native ad networks for another company.

One day, as it was becoming clear that Kevin was better at lead gen for the ad networks than his core duties, his then-boss and still-friend told him to take the afternoon off and see if he could get enough clients to run his own agency. Kevin called and emailed five former clients, all of whom had offered him jobs, and they all signed up to be his clients that same day. Six weeks later, Kevin asked his old colleague at iProspect, John Pellinghelli, to come on to run SEM while he ran Facebook. Metric Digital was born.

From John's perspective, having risen the ranks at a Dentsu-Aegis search agency (iProspect), he saw firsthand how becoming part of a holding company began to keep his office from thriving. His division's profitability was used to shore up losses in other divisions, keeping them from hiring and delivering the value their clients paid them for.

At the same time, their own profitability was increased by packaging hidden costs into media and billing it to clients as "tracking fees," of which 5% was the real cost and the remaining 95% was margin for the agency. Compared to the programmatic world, this was one of the more benign acts of markup deception.

Above all, John watched what was once an innovative company slowing in adoption of emerging channels like social media and native ads. Innovation stopped happening, clients expected more, but they were delivering less. His agency's high minimum fees and the emergence of the D2C market revealed an opportunity to create an agency for an underserved market that was ready to grow.

Joining Kevin at Metric Digital was a no-brainer.

Finally, Ryan Markman came aboard to complete our executive leadership team. Ryan began his career as a management consultant for Bain & Company, advising Fortune 1000 clients on growth strategy, operational improvements, and mergers and acquisitions. His experience as GM of Boostable, a Y Combinator-backed advertising platform for small businesses, exposed him to the complex challenges and remarkable opportunities of the digital advertising industry. A recovering management consultant with adtech startup experience, Ryan joined John and Kevin to build a digital marketing agency that adds transparent business value for its clients.

Fast forward to today, and our firm has become the go-to expert for driving scalable growth for direct-to-consumer companies. Metric Digital has grown from a team of 5 at the end of 2016 to a team of about 25 at the end of 2018. Today, our firm has become a market leader in creating profit- driven growth for companies big and small. Since its inception, Metric Digital has driven hundreds of millions of dollars for clients that mostly came in through referrals from existing clients.

In short: We were trying to build an agency that we were proud of. One that could get brands the results they wanted in a transparent way, and one that could still have fun while doing it.

We have a long way to go, but we're proud of where we are today.

Unfortunately, not every marketing agency in the industry held the same philosophy...

PART 1: HISTORICAL CONTEXT

"We're still in the early stages of a massive shift to digital marketing that people think we finished years ago."

-Kevin Simonson

DOES YOUR MARKETING AGENCY SUCK?

"I hated my last agency."

We hear this far too often from potential clients. And it's a double-edged sword for us.

One the one hand, it's positive, because the bar is low and we have an opportunity to completely outperform the client's expectations.

On the other hand, it's negative because poor experiences can poison a company's view of all marketing agencies and clients become rightfully defensive.

So why is this so common?

Three words: Unhealthy agency relationships.

From a historical context, let's unpack badvertising by diving into the five problems that have caused so many of the toxic client relationships we hear about today:

1. Agencies sell services they don't actually know how to fulfill

2. Structural problems that limit agency adaptability

3. Lack of focus on or intentional clouding of results

4. Contract length and pricing

5. Transparency and account access

Problem #1: Agencies sell services they don't actually know how to fulfill

When you are a marketing agency, clients will often ask you:

"I know you do X (e.g., web design), but can you also do Y (e.g., Facebook ads)?"

Thinking about making a short-term dollar, lots of agencies will say yes to Y, regardless of whether they truly have those capabilities in-house. This leads to agencies selling services that they have no business offering.

"Of course we can do that for your company! Quick, have our intern google 'email marketing strategies.'"

This is especially harmful in the paid performance advertising world. If you have someone inexperienced running your paid marketing, you can lose lots of money, quickly.

We believe that agencies should only sell the services where they have strong capabilities; as such, we are decidedly not a full-service agency. A full-service agency is typically a jack of all trades and master of none. We are experts in using paid advertising and email marketing, and to make companies more money. We're not a full-service agency, and we don't play one on the internet.

A lot of agencies pretend to be full-service agencies where they're doing twelve different things, but they're really one guy outsourcing all the other work to other agencies. You're just getting charged more as the end client because they're going to take a margin.

This isn't an inherently evil thing, but it is usually very opaque to the end client. If white labeling or outsourcing is going on, brands should at least know that this is going on. And again, if you think you need a full-service agency, you might actually be working with four agencies and not realize it.

Beware of the full-service agencies. They're notorious for responding to the client request of, "Hey, can you do this?" with "Sure!" and then just winging it. Whereas saying no and sticking to the services they're good at, would be the fairer thing to do. Agencies should hold transparency conversations with clients and partners, becoming the types of companies who will say no, as opposed to taking another dollar no matter what.

Problem #2: Structural problems that limit agency adaptability

Let's continue with a little background. The agency world has undergone tons of consolidation in the past several decades. Today, most medium to large agencies are owned by one of the Big Five agency holding companies: Publicis Groupe, Interpublic Group, Omnicom, WPP, or Dentsu-Aegis.

The five horsemen of the marketing agency apocalypse, so to speak.

The holding companies manage their portfolio companies for slow to medium growth, but in a rapidly growing industry that requires constant innovation, this can be a huge problem.

Adweek recently reported on WPP cutting 3,500 jobs to refocus on creative and data with no more agency mergers, quoting an agency executive who said, "digital is a word that has been banned from our agency. That artificial distinction between analog and digital is not helpful."

Also, a former EVP at a Big Five-owned ad agency recently told us, *"The holding companies won't let their agencies lose money in the short term, so they can't invest in the future."*

He went on to explain that this strategy is a huge problem in a changing marketplace, as these agencies still derive a large portion of their revenue from shrinking industries like print advertising.

Big agencies thus focus too much on areas they have traditionally made money from, and haven't innovated out of, leading them to fall behind in areas of growth like digital advertising. And even though they are often weak in digital advertising, these agencies still own "agency of record" relationships at major companies, causing them to either:

1. Execute subpar work in digital and disappoint their clients, or

2. Outsource the work to smaller agencies, while the end client doesn't know the labor is being outsourced and their agency of record is marking up someone else's work.

Big agencies can also struggle to attract and retain top talent, as these rising stars often want to be on the cutting edge.

"The big companies move too slow. Smart digital people, if they stay at one of the Big Five agencies, they become digitally stupid people. Smart people are leaving," said the aforementioned executive.

Ultimately, advertising holding companies have tried to become low risk, low growth, stability oriented, and thus short term entities, although they mostly aren't succeeding at doing so. They *want* all of their portfolio companies to deliver consistent growth in revenue and profit. Problem is, they're in a world that's rapidly changing and they're not well equipped to compete in it.

These huge companies historically have done great things, but now aren't thriving with the newer, more important things. That's a major evolution. What they need to do is totally blow up that model and invest in things like digital where they don't have capabilities. Their holding companies won't allow them to do that. They say: "Hey, hold on to every print dollar, you can hold on to every radio dollar that you can!"

That's why a lot of performance marketing agencies have popped up in the last five to ten years. They serve these nascent needs that the larger agencies struggle with. Like Facebook advertising, Google Adwords, and so on.

That's why the Big Five are buying smaller agencies or constantly taking their own people to spin up new ones. They can keep selling their existing relationships something that's not stale.

The agencies that thrive are the ones for whom freedom and encouragement to innovate are a huge part of their culture. Firms who aggressively try new things and test the unproven to solve problems, win. And so do their clients.

Problem #3: Lack of focus on or intentional clouding of results

Attend a conference for vendors in the digital marketing industry, and you will hear tons of stories about Fortune 500 clients throwing digital marketing dollars down the drain.

And understandably, if you want to be a good marketer, you're going to lose money testing things that don't work. We're not saying that's bad. It's okay to lose money. You should lose money. That means you're testing and trying new things.

The questions are 1) whether the new things you're trying are being measured properly and 2) if the agency is trying to drive results for the client, or pull the wool over their eyes.

Think back to one of the vignettes in our opening chapter. An agency we met was bragging about their high digital spend for essentially shoddy work, and sitting around the table laughing about how they blew $6 million on ads without even knowing where those ads showed up.

This tends to happen more frequently for companies that focus on impressions, instead of sales or some other target. If your KPI is maximizing ad impressions, your agency will get you cheap impressions. Do they drive results? Probably not. If they aren't measured on the performance of those impressions, they likely won't deliver performance.

Don't believe us? Check out this quote from the CEO of one of the largest marketing agencies in the world, Dentsu Aegis:

"The agency world needs to lean more into the world of performance, where the value of creativity, impact of strategy and flawlessness of execution means we're demonstrating real business results."

He knows it's coming and they need to change. Digital advertising has brought with it an ability to track almost everything. Previously, this wasn't possible. You could run a newspaper or television ad, but attributing sales to that ad was very difficult.

Unfortunately, many agencies and internal marketing departments haven't evolved to this reality, and treat marketing as if we are still in a TV, radio, and print world. Measuring reach but not profits of their campaigns.

Darren Herman, a former agency and ad tech entrepreneur and current operating partner at Bain Capital, has seen this firsthand. He leads the whitespace that exists between marketing, advertising, content, and technology.

"Major CPG companies are still happy today because they get 192 million impressions at a $4.52 CPM, but we need to push marketing departments towards measuring outcomes. Companies must move from viewing marketing departments as an cost center to a profit center," says Herman.

Compounding this issue, there is not yet an accepted gold standard of tracking. A savvy agency can manipulate real data to show the appearance of financial success.

To avoid this, we recommend agencies set financial goals and benchmarks ahead of time, and agree with clients on how performance will be tracked. We'll talk about this in greater detail later in the book.

Sadly, too many agencies are not performance-oriented. They don't even really know how to track digital marketing in the most granular way. They may not even know that their performance is wrong. Meanwhile, their clients are getting bad results. And they can just say, "Hey, here are the ads we made, enjoy."

Problem #4: Contract length and pricing

Once you've seen a ghost, you're always afraid of the dark. Similarly, once a business has had multiple bad experiences with marketers, price and contract length tend to be scrutinized and incorrectly evaluated. Burned buyers tend to look in the wrong direction, viewing the shorter contracts and cheaper price points as a plus.

Generally, most quality marketing firms worth their salt will want to enter into a longer-term agreement with brands, typically three months or more. This type of agency is taking the longer view, rather than a short-term and inevitably short-lived payday.

After a few bad experiences, it's entirely reasonable to want a month-to-month contract to minimize risk, but typically these don't play out as promised. It takes time, skill, and patience to effectively launch a paid campaign that produces consistent returns. There's a lot of work to do in month one of an agency contract, but in a month-to-month contract you incentivize your agency to spend disproportionate time and effort convincing you that things are moving in the right direction instead of building a foundation for sustainable, profitable growth.

Conversely, super-long contracts are not the answer either. Locking your capital up for that length of time is dangerous because it fails to create any urgency on the part of the agency. Even if they ramp it up in the latter half of the contract duration, why tie your money up for a year in what boils down to four months of quality work?

You want terms that are reasonable. Multi-year contracts are too long, but fewer than 3 months tends to encourage myopic thinking.

The same goes for price. If a marketing agency is willing to cut to bargain basement levels, the real management cost is so small that there probably isn't any skills-based management going on at all. The pricing of the services should reflect their overall value. It's best to do some comparative shopping and, if you're being offered pricing that seems too good to be true, understand that it probably is. Also note that if an agency is charging a low fee, they will likely need to have one account manager handling a ton of clients to make their economics work. Remember, price is what you pay, value is what you get.

Entering into an a slightly longer, pricier agreement may take more consideration, but is the best way to align incentives. It forces your agency to put in their best work, yielding you a better ROI. In exchange the agency gets a consistent and healthy balance sheet. This is the best type of agreement to keep both parties vested in the success of the campaign. It's the equivalent of telling the agency "there's more where that came from." Now they must earn it.

Problem #5: Transparency and account access

Last but certainly not least, we see far too many agencies who won't even give their Fortune 500 clients access to their Facebook and Adwords accounts. The norm for many digital advertising client-agency relationships is for the agency, not the client, to own the advertising accounts in Facebook, Google, and more. These are the accounts where all the digital advertising work happens. Agencies do this for a few reasons:

1. It makes it much harder for the client to leave. If the client leaves, they lose all of the advertising work and data in the agency-owned account. Agencies should retain clients by adding value, not by putting up walls that don't let clients out.

2. It allows the agency to limit what the client can access, and thus limits the client's ability to hold the agency accountable. The agency controls the narrative of what is happening within the client's digital advertising – what ads are running, how they are performing, and where are they showing. Best case scenario, an agency who limits the client's account access is providing great, transparent reporting and insights on their work in some other fashion. Worst case scenario, the agency is spinning a false narrative about their work and hiding what is really going on. Either way, there's no great argument on why a client shouldn't access their advertising accounts.

In other words, agencies do this entirely for their own benefit.

This is unacceptable to us. It's a strategy for retaining clients by putting up walls and hiding work, and thus is completely shortsighted.

We believe brands should not only have access to their ad accounts; they should own them. This lack of transparency is, in our opinion, a bigger problem than ad fraud and leads to more money being wasted.

Our advice to brand-side marketers: insist that your company own your digital advertising accounts. By owning your accounts, you will set a foundation for a better agency relationship and more long-term success.

Ultimately, we see these five problems with the current agency landscape as areas of massive opportunity. That's the good news for marketing executives, and for small marketing agencies. As the Big Five agencies show signs of weakness, the next wave of nimble, results-oriented agencies are rising to drive innovation, growth, and profitability for brands. But only if companies are ready.

WHO IS MOST AFFECTED BY BADVERTISING?

Badvertising affects a lot of different types of companies (and people at those companies) in myriad ways.

When we're considering the impact of badvertising, we like to consider several main archetypes.

Let's flesh each of those out with specific examples of how badvertising affects them, in both the short and long term.

**Please note that while these are generalizations, if you identify with any one of these roles, it may be time to think about how badvertising might be affecting your company's marketing performance.

The first two archetypes show up on the brand side:

1. Entrepreneur
Startup CEO, Founder, or Co-Founder

One badvertising experience can completely turn this persona off to digital. This can completely cripple their ability to scale their business. It can be the difference between getting off the ground and being successful, and not. The effects are profound.

One of the understandable ways that small startup entrepreneurs encounter badvertising is by going with whoever is cheapest. For example, a vendor who is doing their SEO tells the entrepreneur that they will buy their Facebook ads for another grand. And it just doesn't go well. That gets the owner into a revolving door situation where marketing service providers are coming through for the wrong reasons.

It's certainly not ad fraud, but it is poor work. And as Kevin's mentor once said, price is what you pay, value is what you get.

If you're a small brand, beware the trap of focusing solely on price when it comes to your digital marketing. Badvertising might be right around the corner.

2. Enterprise Buyer
   Director of Digital, Senior Executive at Fortune 1000 Brand

Imagine your giant ad agency is doing a poor job at digital marketing. This happens a lot. And the short term effect is, your company misses out on opportunities to generate significant revenue and turn marketing into a profit center. The long term impact of this type of badvertising is that is you lose significant share to upstart growth brands: if you're not doing what you should be doing properly, then there's a void to fill, and somebody faster and smaller will steal your market share.

One "timely" example comes to mind.

Five to seven years ago in the watch industry, most large brands weren't doing direct-to-consumer marketing well. And so new upstarts like MVMT came in and ate their lunch. But if the legacy brands had been there and been competitive in the spaces that MVMT used, i.e., Facebook, Reddit, influencers, Pinterest and search, they could've crushed the competition. And part of the blame for this falls on the digital agencies for these existing brands, who did not push their clients to innovate.

As an enterprise professional, it's imperative that you hold your agency accountable. Make sure you're asking the right paid social questions and email marketing questions, so you create the highest leverage for your brand.

Our second two archetypes exist on the business-to-business side of things:

3. Agencies & Tech Companies
Account Managers and Service Providers

While the first two archetypes are only *affected* by badvertising, the second two are both affected by and creators of badvertising. And for these players, internal badvertising = churn.

This happens primarily at agencies that are effective at selling, but not skilled at delivering. They get employees in who then leave twelve months later. Now, some businesses do really well with this approach, but it's not a long-term model. Particularly in today's climate where people are asking more and more of the right questions, questions that draw on experience and longevity, as we referenced above.

Please note, this is usually a problem with leadership either understaffing and/or under training, rather than employees just performing poorly. We believe there are smart, capable and hardworking people that sometimes get stuck in bad situations. If you're one of those people, come find us, because working at a bad agency or ad tech firm is bad for you too.

And as for the tech companies like programmatic display networks, the market is clearly moving to transparency. Seb Joseph from Digiday recently published an article on the evolving agency-client relationship, saying the following:

"Accountability is front of mind for most big brands as corporate-wide pressure to save costs hits marketing departments. Marketers, in order to prevent budgets being cut, need to know how much of their media buys actually work. Clients are seeing through the games being played. They can see the ROI on digital right there on their dashboards."

If you're a technology platform, and your business model is built off of intentionally obscuring, aka fraud, then the market is moving against you. Either get used to losing those margins with your business, or create a better product that's going to better serve people.

Thankfully, companies like Moat and DoubleVerify are leading the charge in ad fraud prevention. Even those tools themselves have had a history of being tricked. But the industry is wising up, forcing the display platforms themselves to actually build in user journey tracking.

Whether you're an agency, or a vendor who provides ad tech to agencies and the brands they serve, you need to think long term. Read our column on the Shopify Partner Blog (www.bit.ly/badvert) about how you can differentiate your marketing agency through radical transparency.

4. Investors
Private Equity, Venture Capital, and other Investing Professionals

As an investor, your goal is to add value to companies, usually measured in revenue, so badvertising affects you by hurting the value of your investments in two major ways.

First, money spent on agencies that commit badvertising is inefficient. The client is paying more for a baseline amount of service than they should.

Maybe the company you have invested in has a certain digital advertising strategy in place because the person dictating the strategy is negligent. The company might think they have reached a point of diminished returns for new customer acquisition for a specific channel (e.g. Facebook).

But it's more likely that they're not using that channel efficiently. Point being, badvertising makes a growth channel less profitable.

Investors are particularly interesting stakeholders because they are objective when it comes to company politics. They have more power to affect change than most people inside the system because they're somewhat an impartial third party. They're clearly invested in the outcome of the business, but they're not so much invested in the egos of the people running the business. Also, they're more binary with respect to what they value in terms of black and white numbers, versus the grays of making people happy.

If you're on the investor, venture capital, or private equity side, lead with your dispassionate outside view. Instead of allowing badvertising to thrive via negligence, hold your brands accountable. Assure performance marketing continues to be focused on the numbers.

Did you see which of the four buckets you fit into? Awesome. Just know this. We approach this book's strategies and tactics through these four lenses for one simple reason:

To create a rising tide that lifts all boats in the digital marketing industry.

All aboard mates. It's time to set sail, navigate the badvertising storm, take back control, and help your company get to the next level. As transparently as possible.

◆ ◆ ◆

Have you been badvertised? Take the quiz to find out.

Considering what you've read so far, do you think you or your company has been a victim of badvertising? Or worse yet, a perpetrator of badvertising?

You're not alone. That's why we've put together a helpful assessment. Answer the following questions to gauge your experience in the digital marketing landscape. This will give you a sense of where you might need to seek improvements, and how you might be poised to grow in the future. You can also take the quiz online or share with team members at www.badvertisingagency.com.

I know how much of my budget my agency spends on ads.

- ☐ Agree Totally
- ☐ Agree Somewhat
- ☐ Neither Agree nor Disagree
- ☐ Disagree Somewhat
- ☐ Strongly Disagree

I know all the locations where my ads are being placed.

- ☐ Agree Totally
- ☐ Agree Somewhat
- ☐ Neither Agree nor Disagree
- ☐ Disagree Somewhat
- ☐ Strongly Disagree

I have access to my advertising accounts.

- ☐ Agree Totally
- ☐ Agree Somewhat
- ☐ Neither Agree nor Disagree
- ☐ Disagree Somewhat
- ☐ Strongly Disagree

I have ownership of my advertising accounts.

- ☐ Agree Totally
- ☐ Agree Somewhat
- ☐ Neither Agree nor Disagree
- ☐ Disagree Somewhat
- ☐ Strongly Disagree

I trust in the accuracy and completeness of the data presented.

- ☐ Agree Totally
- ☐ Agree Somewhat
- ☐ Neither Agree nor Disagree
- ☐ Disagree Somewhat
- ☐ Strongly Disagree

I believe my account manager optimizes at every opportunity.

- ☐ Agree Totally
- ☐ Agree Somewhat
- ☐ Neither Agree nor Disagree
- ☐ Disagree Somewhat
- ☐ Strongly Disagree

I feel confident with the health of my current agency relationship.	☐ Agree Totally ☐ Agree Somewhat ☐ Neither Agree nor Disagree ☐ Disagree Somewhat ☐ Strongly Disagree
I receive easy and organized tracking for my campaigns.	☐ Agree Totally ☐ Agree Somewhat ☐ Neither Agree nor Disagree ☐ Disagree Somewhat ☐ Strongly Disagree
I have access to real time data and insights about my campaigns.	☐ Agree Totally ☐ Agree Somewhat ☐ Neither Agree nor Disagree ☐ Disagree Somewhat ☐ Strongly Disagree
My agency is up-to-date on marketing trends that impact my campaigns.	☐ Agree Totally ☐ Agree Somewhat ☐ Neither Agree nor Disagree ☐ Disagree Somewhat ☐ Strongly Disagree
I have an agency contract that is flexible with my changing needs.	☐ Agree Totally ☐ Agree Somewhat ☐ Neither Agree nor Disagree ☐ Disagree Somewhat ☐ Strongly Disagree
My agency is doing the work, not secretly outsourcing to someone else.	☐ Agree Totally ☐ Agree Somewhat ☐ Neither Agree nor Disagree ☐ Disagree Somewhat ☐ Strongly Disagree

I can engage with my account manager thoughtfully and honestly.	☐ Agree Totally ☐ Agree Somewhat ☐ Neither Agree nor Disagree ☐ Disagree Somewhat ☐ Strongly Disagree
I have defined goals for each agency service my company hired.	☐ Agree Totally ☐ Agree Somewhat ☐ Neither Agree nor Disagree ☐ Disagree Somewhat ☐ Strongly Disagree
My agency engages in projects that are transparent and focused on results.	☐ Agree Totally ☐ Agree Somewhat ☐ Neither Agree nor Disagree ☐ Disagree Somewhat ☐ Strongly Disagree
I believe my agency only recommends services we need most.	☐ Agree Totally ☐ Agree Somewhat ☐ Neither Agree nor Disagree ☐ Disagree Somewhat ☐ Strongly Disagree
My agency's approach is customized and not "one size fits all."	☐ Agree Totally ☐ Agree Somewhat ☐ Neither Agree nor Disagree ☐ Disagree Somewhat ☐ Strongly Disagree

See results below! Do most of your answers...

Strongly Disagree? Get out now.

You are a victim of badvertising. It may not be your fault, but it's your responsibility to part company with your agency and find a more responsible marketing partner.

Disagree Somewhat? There's room for improvement.

Nobody's perfect, but now is the time to begin holding your agency more accountable. If they don't deliver greater transparency soon, consider seeking other options.

Agree Somewhat? Keep up the good work.

Sounds like you have a healthy agency relationship. Well done. Make sure that level of transparency and productivity continues!

Agree Totally? You've found a transparent agency.

Congratulations, you have built a healthy and fruitful relationship with your marketing partner that's based on real results. Hold onto that agency!

Next, here's how to find the right agency and, more importantly, how to spot the wrong one.

PART 2: CURRENT LANDSCAPE

"You shine a light in a dark place to find out what's going on. Now that brands are asking for transparency with their agencies, that's what's happening, and brands are finding that they're being lied to."

-Kevin Simonson

WHERE IS DIGITAL MARKETING TODAY?

Despite where digital marketing has arrived, we're skeptical, but not cynical.

We're extremely encouraged about its next phase of evolution. We certainly wish it would go faster, but then again, we would say that about most things.

And we're not alone. Andrew Essex, former CEO of Droga5, published a compelling book in 2017, *The End of Advertising*, that shared both our optimism and our skepticism.

"Unlike many naysayers, I'm actually optimistic about what will take the place of traditional advertising, about the brave new landscape that lies ahead. On the other hand, I'm brutally realistic about entropy, and how hard it will be to bring this dying industry back from the brink."

Essex is probably the highest-profile person who put that much dedication into a singular message about how badvertising is all coming to an end.

Point is, people are listening. Increased turnover is causing companies to question what's been done, and move over to newer, smarter, and more results-oriented marketing programs.

◆ ◆ ◆

As a result of the evolution of modern business, there are now a few different challenges we're up against in the digital marketing industry.

The first challenge to point out is account access.

Here's a story about one of our Fortune 500 clients (name withheld to honor confidentiality), about where badvertising and reporting collide

Prior to working with us, their Big Five agency set up an ad account for them, but it wasn't actually the one they were using. When we got inside, we discovered there was nothing in there. It was like giving a little kid a toy steering wheel so he can feel like he's moving. Or like giving your little brother an unplugged controller when he wants to crash a video game. They had access to *an* account but not *the* account. This example intermingles both of the badvertising categories (ad fraud and incompetence).

Now, as a businessperson, you can see the benefit of restricting access. Doing so means it would be harder for a client to fire you if they can't see what you're doing. Certain agencies could think of it as a customer retention tool, but so is kidnapping. They're intentionally hiding what they're doing and they're getting retention by putting up walls and tricking the client rather than providing value.

Other problems can come from a lack of understanding about attribution. There are still a lot of big agencies that are geared towards just getting clients to buy stuff. Their reporting rests on an ability to spend your ad budget on time, and then simply report back on the impressions. And it's kind of inexcusable to focus on that when you could instead be tracking conversions. On top of that, lots of big agencies and big brands still want to find the cheapest impressions, even though not all impressions are created equal, resulting in imprecise, impersonal mass outreach.

Stories like these coined one of our joking taglines at Metric Digital:

"We're the agency you hire after the agency you fire."

But what happens when brands show up tattered and torn from previous toxic relationships?

Here's what we see when we work with them every day: Clearly, many companies that come to us have had a negative experience, particularly the smaller brands. Because with agencies, there is a certain amount clients have to spend in order to get service.

In order to set proper expectations and create a plan that works internally and externally, as an agency we need to have a frank conversation about why brands have had those experiences and how to make sure they don't happen again. However, by the time a brand has already gone to three agencies involved in bad-faith practices, then seek us out as the fourth, it's an uphill battle. They're usually also considering internal hires for the marketing work because they think that could give them the control they lacked with the previous agencies.

It happens all the time.

Much of this mishandling comes from clients just getting thrown into the same system that a thousand other companies are getting thrown into, so there's no customization. This might work for some companies, but not all of them. Yes, we think technology is only going to continually continue to be a bigger and bigger part of how performance marketing is managed. But it's also often used as a smokescreen for impersonal account service.

"Just use our proprietary algorithm," some agencies say. But it's often nothing that sophisticated. Agencies just can't afford to have people providing custom service. They're charging far too low of rate. They can't have actual people who are actually doing the work.

Machine learning and technology will be a huge part of the continued evolution of digital marketing. But it breaks our heart that marketing agencies are hiding behind a mirage.

Because that affects everyone in the industry. Including you.

To wrap up this chapter, we wanted to share one final digital marketing story. Kevin calls this tale, "I Was Your Facebook Proprietary Ad Tech."

I went to pitch a client with my boss, and learned something that would fundamentally change the way I thought about how marketing agencies work.

He was the CEO of the Facebook marketing agency I worked at. We used proprietary ad technology to help us get better results on Facebook than our competitors, agencies who didn't use our ad tech.

Kind of.

Our team consisted of several engineers that built the tech; and myself, the Facebook ads expert, who ran everything for the clients.

My boss would overpromise and I'd explain how we would try and deliver.

In this meeting, he told clients that our agency had proprietary tech that would give us a performance edge over our competition because we had an algorithm that would identify the top performing creative, derive insights, and then make recommendations on what creative we should iterate to continue to improve performance over time.

The client signed on the spot and we went back to our office.

As we were walking back down Madison Ave (I wish I was joking) I naively asked my boss about this creative recommendation algorithm that made us better than the competition, as I had no idea the engineers had been working on this.

After breaking out in laughter he stopped, looked at me, and said, "Kevin, **you're** the proprietary algorithm."

As I've gotten older, wiser, and experienced working with more agencies, I've learned that this is the way the marketing agency world works.

Technology helps us be more efficient, better marketers, but the vast majority of what agencies sell to brands is a flat out lie. They do this because, at least in the short term, the lie works and closes deals.

Here's proof. It's like Mad Libs for pitching:

Step 1: "We're a team founded by ex Google/Facebook Engineers."

Step 2: "We've built proprietary algorithms/technology that identifies/optimizes bidding/creative."

Step 3: "AI/Machine Learning"

Step 4: "We can only show you these screenshots and can't disclose further information because it's proprietary."

It gets old.

I see the same ad accounts from the same agencies that make that same pitch all the time because they churn after their contract ends.

You can't obfuscate revenue forever and the smart brands eventually realize why they're plateauing or not getting the results they were promised.

"The algorithm needs more time/data to optimize properly," says their rep.

Nope, it doesn't. You're just lying.

Metric Digital uses technology that we've built that helps us drive incremental revenue. Is it proprietary tech? Yes. Is it ultimately why you should work with us? No.

To avoid this badvertising nightmare, be sure you work with marketing agencies that have a track record of success and a client page of brands that you aspire to be like. Talk to those brands on their client pages and ask them about their results working with that agency.

Don't settle for screenshots or "we can't share that with you because it's proprietary" answers.

Otherwise you might end up being another brand we talk to that churned through the same agencies that gave the same pitches and had the same bad outcomes.

PART 3: STRATEGY & TACTICS

"If the agency is not doing everything in their power to help brands optimize, then why are they there?"

-John Pellinghelli

WHAT ARE THE QUESTIONS YOU SHOULD BE ASKING YOUR FACEBOOK MARKETING AGENCY?

Finding the right marketing agency for your company is hard, but keeping them honest is even harder. In this section, we're going to equip you with the right questions to ask your Facebook, Search, and Email agencies.

Starting with Facebook, here are some patterns we see a lot of:

- Marketing agencies that "Do Facebook"

- Facebook marketing gurus

- Facebook anti-guru gurus who tell you not to trust gurus because they are the real experts

- Content about how an Agency/Guru/Anti-Guru does Facebook marketing

We have begrudgingly accepted that we're not going to stop any of this.

But you can ask agencies and "expert" Facebook marketers the right questions. You can suss out if they really are good at Facebook marketing, or just good at talking about it.

Richard Feynman famously talked about the difference between knowing the name of something and actually knowing something:

"Names don't constitute knowledge. Simply knowing the name of something, like a bird, for example, is not the same as knowing how that bird flies or finds its way. Even if you can translate the word for bird into five languages, it didn't mean you know anything."

Experiential knowledge, then, is sound judgment, relevant insight and meaningful perspective. Whereas nominal knowledge is more like an intern googling "Facebook Advertising Tips" during a conference call.

Here are the questions you can ask to tell the difference:

"How do you define Cost Per Acquisition (CPA) as it applies to Facebook?"

This is the quintessential metric for determining the return on your investment. Most companies consider CPA to be their top metric. But since the answer to every marketing questions is, "well, it depends," it all comes down to your average revenue per customer. Know this number going into every agency meeting or call.

Here's more about how we answer this question, using ecommerce as an example:

At its most basic level, blended Facebook CPA is Facebook ad spend divided by the number of sales driven by those Facebook ads. However, keeping things this high level will obscure some of what is really going on.

To get a better picture, you should also break down CPA the following ways:

- CPA for existing customers
- CPA for new customers (you should be willing to pay more for a new customer, based on the customer's expected lifetime value)
    - New customer prospecting CPA (e.g. introducing new people to the brand)
    - New customer remarketing CPA (e.g. targeting someone with an ad who has never purchased but has added an item to cart)

Oftentimes, blended CPA will hide unprofitable new customer acquisition costs.

To get technical for a moment, CPA stands for Cost Per Acquisition, although this number usually gets intermixed and measured as a general Cost Per Order. Typically, most companies refer to CPA as an order, and a new customer CPA as CAC (Customer Acquisition Cost).

"What attribution window do you use and why?"

This is by far the most missed question to dive into when talking to any performance marketer on any channel. The default attribution window is 28 days post-click and 1 day post-view. In all of our audits, we use it as a default on our dashboards. But the default is not the only thing companies should look at. We recommend looking at other attribution windows as well to better understand how that can affect your interpretation of channel performance, using for example 7-day click or no-view-through.

"What Facebook campaign objectives do you use and how do they work together to increase customers and revenue under a set CPA? Why?"

Since your goals are bottom of the funnel, acquisition- and revenue-based, it's important to make sure your agency isn't wholly distracted by the top-of-funnel blue-sky world of brand awareness. That objective has its merits, but they are secondary to your immediate goals. So ask this question to prevent your company from getting to the top of the ladder only to find you're leaning against the wrong digital wall.

"How do you structure your account to address prospective new customers? Customers who have never seen the brand on Facebook, seen and/or interacted with the brand on Facebook, or already purchased from my brand? Why?"

At a minimum, the account should have separate campaigns for new customer prospecting, new customer remarketing, and existing customers. Every campaign is modified based on how much your target customers know, like, and trust you. And every piece of online real estate counts. Even the call-to-action button. For example, new customers are more likely to click on copy reading, "Learn More," and "Explore," as opposed to prequalified buyers who click on language like "Buy Now" and "Subscribe." Make sure your agency chooses wisely.

"What is an optimal amount of audience overlap across ad sets for prospecting, retargeting, and retention? Why do you think so, and what factors would cause you to change your mind?"

The above is a tough question, which is why we ask it. There are two ways to look at it: the idealist and the pragmatic. We'll start with a pragmatic. If something's working, you should do it. If you have high audience overlap for retargeting ads and your goals are being hit, it's not wrong.

But the idealist always says, how could things be better? Good is never good enough. So where do you experiment? You could focus on numbers; for example, we don't want our audience overlap to ever be more than 60%. What you're seeing across all your accounts should dictate the actual percentages you paid for.

From an audience overlap perspective, you should start by separating first-time visitors; those who have engaged with the brand before; those who have been to the site but haven't bought; and retaining those who have. The volume of the account would dictate how you break it out at the campaign or ad set level. Then you can get more tactical by having two processes in place to make sure that any overlaps are sealed tight: (1) automatically updating lists, and (2) excluding based on site visitors, depending on how you segment. Those should be measured separately because they're doing different things.

The second part of this final question is also important. Some agencies are open minded to humility in the abstract, but in reality, it's a trait often perceived as a sign of weakness. If you're paying your agency $15,000 a month, then you have the right to push back on their advice and have a real conversation. Perhaps invite them to change their mind when new information arises. Be persistent. Be overly organized. Set expectations as a client.

"Do you include or exclude any placements or devices in your targeting? If so, which ones and why?"

Idealists would say you should always test new things to see if there's room for improvement. Placements should depend on user behavior and how they are interacting with the brand online. But obviously the bottom line—the pragmatic side—is always ROI. There are certain verticals like food subscription and personal care, businesses that people engage with on the history of organically you tend to see sometimes in cases split placements, specifically facebook, instagram. But generally speaking, auto placements is still the way to go now. I'm sure that will change like all this stuff changes in some way. That's why you have to be on the forefront of it.

"What types of creative assets do you recommend we start with? Do you have any requests for certain types of creative assets? Why?"

The feedback you get here is an ideal start for what could lead to deeper questions regarding Facebook marketing expertise. These are virtually the same questions we ask when interviewing a Senior Facebook Marketer for our agency.

(On a related note, for the ins and outs of Facebook creative from the people who actually run it, check out our Ad Creative Playbook [www.bit.ly/metricdigital1]. It's a helpful resource to drive more revenue, optimize every ad placement, to test, and to respond to audiences for every objective.)

A final note on holding a Facebook agency or guru to the fire:

An actual Facebook marketing expert will give examples explaining their responses to each of the above questions. We find that experiential expertise is key when it comes to Facebook, because the "right answer" varies widely depending on contextual variables that should also be teased out.

In other words, most businesses have nuances that will impact what the proper Facebook marketing strategy will be, and an expert Facebook marketer will be able to address those nuances.

To wrap up, another quote from Richard Feynman:

"For a successful technology, reality must take precedence over public relations, for nature cannot be fooled."

Just remember, the larger your agency is, the more perception management is important for them. Clients should be mindful of who's handling their account during onboarding, and their attunement to the nuance described above.

You can tell if you're getting quality service right away by asking some key questions. The key to achieving transparency is doing so as early as possible.

WHAT ARE THE QUESTIONS YOU SHOULD BE ASKING YOUR SEM AGENCY?

Next up, if your company decides to engage with an SEM agency, there are also several questions to ask yourself and that agency during the vetting process and throughout the relationship.

"How does the agency's strategy align with our company goals?"

Your agency should be digging into what your business objectives are, and asking questions to get at those goals.

For example, many high growth brands prioritize performance marketing spend on the coveted and most difficult to scale, new customer acquisition, aka first time purchasers.

Google can be a highly effective channel for doing this, but the strategy and execution should align with that objective. Follow up questions might include:

- What Google channel tactics are most effective for driving new customers?

- How would you structure your account around acquisition versus retention?

- What three tools are most effective, and the three new things you're most excited about?

The answers to those will change as the platform changes. In general, look for the ability and desire to cleanly segment strategy, spend, and performance reporting by objective. When creating a discrete strategy for driving new customers, you're talking about reaching the unconverted, prioritizing Non-Brand Search and Shopping, mid-funnel Display using Lookalike audiences, and excluding past purchaser audiences.

Driving repeat orders & retention is valuable as well, but companies would do well to separate spend and goals for the retention objective, targeting a higher ROAS, as these customers are not incremental to the brand.

Overall, you want to test how well your agency knows the platform and your goals, and also how much they're testing, pushing the envelope and thinking ahead.

"What is the agency's spend structure?"

If your agency operates on 100% media spend, then there is the obvious incentive for the agency to spend more. This is a good thing if goals and guardrails are clearly defined. You want your agency to be constantly seeking opportunities to scale your spend if that spend is driving profit for you.

You do want to ensure that your agency is seeking growth in areas that will drive incremental growth for your business. Remember, not all revenue is created equal and high ROAS is relative.

For example, if Branded Search is operating at a 10x ROAS and 95% Impression Share, then there is little headroom to push it further. Branded Search is reaching those knowledgeable about the brand and those who have previously converted.

However, an unscrupulous agency could continue bidding higher on Branded Search, driving more spend there while still maintaining high blended ROAS. Despite how Google describes their auction mechanics, we have seen firsthand that Brand costs can spiral out of control if one or more competitor is in the market. Brand Search also tends to be very low maintenance for an agency, with little need for creative or challenging strategy in the same way that the battlefield areas of Non-Brand, Shopping, Display, and YouTube are when you're optimizing for Customer-Acquisition Cost or ROAS.

This question speaks to the need for breaking out performance reporting by Brand and Non-Brand, which your performance agency should be eager to do.

"Where do you see most incremental opportunities?"

Another way to phrase this question is, "If we had an opportunity to push 20% more budget into the channels how would you spend it?"

Even if your campaigns are going well, there will always be opportunities to improve. You want to evaluate whether your agency is thinking ahead and has a finger on the pulse of your account. General answers or blue-sky tests could be red flags. For example, if the agency says, "We'll spend more on what's working" without telling you what that is.

If that answer is "Branded Search," then run. You're likely already maximizing Branded Search and a tactic geared at existing customers. A blue-sky test is "Let's push that money into YouTube" when you have done zero testing there to date. Another bad answer is choosing to spend more on areas that won't scale.

Instead, look for specific ideas that tie to your goals, business trends, and are based on real data, i.e., "We're seeing a great trend in the Yoga Short keyword category and impression share data shows opportunity to spend 5% of that incremental budget there. Let's test increasing bids on that category and building more upper funnel head keywords to drive keyword discovery and first time purchasers."

"What is actually providing real incremental gains, below the surface of revenue growth?"

The revenue, conversion, ROA, or CPA numbers in a platform don't always tell the whole story. If your agency seems to be driving significant revenue but, upon a deeper drill-down you discover that 90% of search revenue is coming from brand search, this signals that a they are less influential than they might appear to be. Customers picked up in brand search (vs. non-brand search) are at least aware of your brand, and there's a good chance that you've already paid elsewhere to acquire them, especially if you're running marketing efforts across other channels. Non-brand acquisitions, on the other hand, are customers that are less aware of your brand, and thus are customers that you're potentially winning over your competition.

If your agency is presenting you a single set of search performance numbers, or a "blended" dataset when you're running both brand and non-brand search, you're not getting the full picture. Badvertising agencies can make a search account look strong and profitable when lower-funnel brand search is actually leading the way.

"What outside audiences are you using to inform or assist your campaigns?

There's a plethora of data available nowadays via remarketing lists for search ads (RLSA), Google Analytics integration, and more to assist the modern Google Ads advertiser. There's raising bids against non-converting site visitors with a higher likelihood to convert than your pure prospecting audiences. There's targeting similar audiences of your highest-value purchasers to cautiously test into new pockets of keywords.

Point being, advertisers are empowered beyond the simple keyword. A good search agency, at the very least, should be leveraging observation bids up against core site audiences. If they're not and are struggling to find optimization solutions beyond "raise the bids," you're not experiencing the full power of the Google Ads platform.

"What's your point of view on account management platforms?"

Any agency worth its digital salt will have an opinion on when such platforms are appropriate, and when they're not. And because these platforms will cost extra, it's imperative to know how useful they will be. Account management platforms can be a way to leverage additional business data, efficiently implement third-party tracking at large scale, or to expand your advertising efforts more effectively into incremental platforms such as Bing and Yahoo Gemini (yes, there are use cases!).

"Is the person I'm meeting going to be the person working on account?"

It's possible that a previous agency sold you one team, but gave you service by another. There's the pitch team and then the actual team. But you have a chance early on in the agency relationship to figure out how to get transparency about the staffing of your account. We believe that for a modern marketing agency to be transparent and successful, they need the right combination of senior leadership and account management. The former—which might include the president and founder of the agency or head of operations—focuses client satisfaction, long term strategy, and overall client business objectives. The latter—which is a pitch—could include a dedicated account management team with a senior specialist for day-to-day execution, short and mid-term strategy, and to be the main point of contact.

"What's your copywriting process?"

If you want to be a little more subtle with the topic of account management, this question will give you greater insight into the agency's approach. Copy can be nuanced. Keywords are easy to figure out, but copy requires a lot of constant testing. Do whatever you can to find out who's writing the copy, how they're testing and iterating it, and how they're uisng data to inform that process.

"How are you demonstrating expertise on the platform?"

Agencies represent a significant marketing expense, and if they're not plugged in to the direction digital trends are going, that's a red flag. You don't want your marketing service provider to be using same techniques they learned five years ago. Find out about their approach to bidding strategies, like whether they prefer manual or automated, and when. Then dig deeper and see if they have use cases for each of those.

This can get highly granular but it's worth taking the time to explore. See if they can figure out how to back into potential available spend and conversions from search impression share, or project spend off a new pocket of keywords that you haven't previously tested. If you'd like to see several examples of using bid strategy to drive conversion for ecommerce brands, visit our blog for several of our recent use cases.

"Where do I need to verify?"

There are many questions you should ask your search agency. But don't forget, there are also questions you shouldn't ask, because due diligence means occasionally diving into your accounts to look for the answers yourself.

For instance, you can ask an agency how frequently they are adjusting bids, but they could say anything. They could have bidding algorithms in place which do all the work. You can always jump into the account and see how frequently bids are being touched by utilizing the change history. Look at the search query report. Be proactive to make sure they're not just blowing smoke and saying what they can to get you off their case.

Remember, there's a difference between performance being good and struggling to break through to the next level, versus performance being bad with the agency telling you something other than what's actually happening. You need to verify.

Ultimately, it's your job to pay attention to information and trends relevant to your brand that your agency might not think of. Keep asking questions. And pay close attention to their responses to see what that says about their character and expertise. Remember, if an agency's solution to everything is "just add in more keywords," then they don't know how to optimize.

WHAT ARE THE QUESTIONS YOU SHOULD BE ASKING YOUR EMAIL MARKETING AGENCY?

If a company decides to engage with an email marketing agency, the most important first step is trust-building. Agencies should always take time to understand the client's brand. They can't just start sending emails.

Now, this differs significantly from hiring a paid advertising or search agency, where you provide brand guidelines and they begin publishing a huge variety of ads to gauge what works.

With email, however, it's a bit more calculated.

Here are the questions to ask yourself and your email marketing agency, both during the vetting process and throughout the relationship itself.

"Can I devote time to managing this agency relationship?"

Brands who engage email marketing agencies must have adequate time and bandwidth in their schedules to equip that vendor with everything they need to win. That means providing guidance on content, insights about inventory, promotions, seasonality, and so on.

Email agencies need to be fed a diverse menu of data and insight in order to create a successful email program. Without those assets, they can't optimize. As the client, be ready to work. Sorry, but you can't hire an email marketing agency and then never think about email again. Quite the opposite. You're actually going to be led through thinking about email more than you've ever thought about it before.

"What are your strategic priorities for growing my business?"

All email agencies should be paying attention to content, audience, and results. Everything they do should fall under one of those three categories. If your agency is not adapting their strategy around these pillars, they're doing your brand a disservice.

Naturally, every agency will have different relationships with different clients. For example, certain brands require more control and input on the final product. But start by making sure these strategic bases are covered.

"Are the agency's tactics working?"

Within the context of where your company was as a whole at the beginning of the agency relationship, your brand should soon see a commensurate lift. Even if the relationship has only existed for a month, they should have already pulled some levers that are going to start to have an impact on revenue.

And note: It's more than simply sending the right emails out. They must also target the right people with the right strategy. And you, as the brand, have the right to ask about that.

"Is my life easier now than it was a month ago?"

Not that it doesn't take work to do email marketing. Substantial conversations are still going to be necessary. You have to stay on top of communication with your vendor. But because email is such a powerful marketing strategy, when executed correctly, your daily marketing life should be at least a little easier.

It's like the classic question candidates ask during presidential elections: "Are you better off than you were four years ago?" If your brand goes too long without being able to answer that question affirmatively, your email marketing agency might be a badvertiser.

"Is there internal pressure that's blocking me from considering all the factors for a successful campaign?"

As the client, when you're in the thick of your daily work, you're probably thinking more about getting your tasks done and less about *how* you're getting them done. You're also thinking more about checking items off your marketing to-do list, since you have other teams nipping at your heels. Which is completely understandable.

Friday afternoon is a good example. If you suddenly decide that you want to send a survey, your email agency might push back on that time and day because of the predictable low open rate. Which you understandably won't be thinking about if you're not thinking about email 100% of the time. But your agency is. Just because you want to check it off your list to relieve internal team pressure, doesn't mean it's the most effective email strategy.

"Have I gotten adequate buy-in from internal players?"

Your brand might have multiple product lines and a robust team. Or highly seasonal products that target certain times of the year. Or even company executives who want to be involved in every stage of the marketing process.

If that's the case, be sure you're representing each of those needs in your regular agency meeting. The last thing you want is to sit down for your weekly call only to realize that you've forgotten to touch base with your product team about their upcoming launch. You don't have to use every one of their suggestions, but getting their input early and often will help them feel included and make you look better in your marketing role.

"Is my email marketing agency a strategic partner, or just a vendor?"

Ideally, your email agency should be challenging you to think beyond just your company's historical consistency. They should be challenging you and your team explore what's new, what needs attention, what's possible. In short, they should be thinking about your company on a true business to business level, rather than just a product level. They should be using strategic marketing leadership to build a foundation for scaling your brand.

❖ ❖ ❖

Remember: Once you've sent an email, you can't take it back.

If you want your email marketing campaigns to become a source of growth revenue, do your due diligence. Ask yourself, your team, and and your agency these questions.

IS YOUR AGENCY HELPING GROW YOUR BUSINESS, OR JUST MAKING YOUR ADS?

Marketing agencies are not obliged to help their clients with forecasting. Every client of every size will require different levels of and approaches to the strategic planning process. We do believe that there are certain patterns to notice around the forecasting process in general.

First, beware agencies who only ever forecast upward, because that's typically going to make them more money. Agencies should be receptive to activities beyond simply trying to get the client to spend more.

Two, keep an eye on credit. What does the agency take credit for? Do they take credit in their forecasting for things that are not truly incremental to their work? Is forecasting actually predicated on, for example, branded search—which has extremely high ROAs—and its attributed revenue? Because branded search builds off of an existing, relatively high intent to buy.

Ultimately, the best marketing agencies are there to be a true partner and help clients grow their businesses, not just make their ads.

In fact, a complaint we often hear about agencies is:

"They're just telling us what to do. There's no strategy. They're not helping us proactively figure out how to grow our account."

The right marketing agency will go above and beyond and help a client through forecasting and through using their strategic voice to unlock scale. Agencies should help clients translate spend into broad, measurable growth.

We believe agencies should be proactively communicating with clients:

"Hey, have you done your forecasting for paid media spend? If not, we can help."

"Here's what you did last year, and here's what the balance should be going forward."

"Here are some models we can use."

That's value added. This kind of agency forecasting helps clients ramp up and acquire. And it means the agency is much more than a mere media buyer, becoming a strategic partner that can deliver holistic business insight.

We believe the most effective agencies will not only hire people with marketing backgrounds, but will hire people with strategy, finance, or math skills who can think critically about holistic growth forecasting.

And not surprisingly, we have an entire library of forecasting guides that we use for our clients' unique goals. But these are only tools. What matters is proactively helping clients pinpoint goals that are challenging, but reasonable.

In your agency relationship, approach your forecasting conversations as tools to empower you to set clear expectations and elevate your marketing team's performance. We'd love to share some of our forecasting tools with you, whether you're a brand or an agency. Email to forecasting@metricdigital.com to request a copy.

IS PROGRAMMATIC ADVERTISING THE RIGHT PATH FOR YOUR BRAND?

Despite all these examples of badvertising, we still have hope.

The demand for clarity, certainty, and trust in online advertising is only becoming more widespread.

Earlier in this book, we mentioned a popular survey from The Association of National Advertisers which notes that just 40% of marketers are comfortable with the level of transparency with their programmatic media investments. The survey also found that 78% of those polled were concerned about brand safety issues in programmatic media buying.

In this next section, we'd like to share our experience and insights around issues related to technology, data, and automation in programmatic media buying.

Let's start simple. At the risk of understating the multibillion dollar digital marketing industry, there are three ways to buy advertising on the internet:

1. You can go to giant platforms where consumers spend a lot of their time, like Facebook, Instagram, and Google.

2. You can partner directly with a particular website that attracts your audience and secure a specific ad inventory.

3. You can use programmatic or demand side platforms that aggregate ad inventory from a variety of websites and use technology to automate media buying.

Each of these approaches is an important part of the industry. But as a performance marketing agency that has spent hundreds of millions of dollars buying ads for a diverse set of ecommerce brands, programmatic should be a lower priority today than Facebook, Instagram, and Google Ads.

We're not bashing programmatic. There is a place for it in digital advertising, especially if your company is looking for additional scale. Our point of view is that it can be valuable as an incremental source for brands that can dedicate a large budget to it. If you are spending less than $1 million on digital advertising a year, you probably won't see extra benefits from also committing time, money, and effort to programmatic advertising.

It's also worth mentioning the impact programmatic has had on the digital marketing industry in the past few years. Our colleague Alice Lee is a veteran in the programmatic space and the founder of Divviup, a technology and marketing consultancy that performs frequent media audits. We asked her about how the industry has shifted, and she had this to say:

"Because of bad actors in the programmatic space, much of the industry and many major brands are now auditing and reviewing agency work, and establishing higher standards of transparency and accountability for their digital media investment.

The brand side wants confirmation and validation, as transparency has been a big buzzword in the last few years. And while some see it as the next shiny object, the trend has pushed a lot of companies like P&G to bring a lot of the trading and media buying in-house.

Another result of the programmatic transparency trend is, brands have started to commission audit work from large consultancies like Deloitte and Accenture, for due diligence on their media agencies. Not surprisingly, those agencies become very defensive. Especially at the Big Five agencies, there is a lot of pushback. What we found is that more boutique agencies demonstrated more agility to support the newfound courage on the brand side, as it helps them differentiate.

Even to this day, it's still very difficult to get data. We found that the contracts that were originally executed by between agencies and brands had a lot of unfavorable language around data ownership for brands."

Alice's point is clear: Brands need to know what they're getting into. And programmatic won't be the right strategy for many of them.

A lot happens in between the moment when you hand over your budget to a trade desk or managed service DSP, and the moment when your ad actually gets served on websites. Frustratingly, that activity is often completely opaque to you. There may be six or seven different programmatic vendors touching the creative and passing it around, unbeknownst to you.

Alice also reminded us that in the current landscape, there might even be thousands of companies between advertisers and publishers—and they all take a cut along the way.

"There are areas where the money disappears and there's no accountability for where the fees went, they just get bundled up into the invoice.

Let's say an agency bills a client $1 million. But when you look at transactional logs, the actual working media cost could be only a fraction of that, say, $400,000.

Media audits uncover surprising ratios. To the point that agencies are not only put on notice, but have had to go through another pitch process to maintain their clients."

As a result of this complex value chain, it's notably hard to track where ads are actually showing up and how they're performing. There is a lack of accountability due to a lack of transparency.

AdLightning said it best in their article about bad ads:

"Display ads often start their journey from agency to audience with one or more quality issues. But those issues are often compounded and new issues are introduced as the ad bounces around in the programmatic machine. And there are no quality checks along the way."

We've seen this happen far too many times. When our agency first engages with a potential or new client, either before a contract is signed or before the kickoff meeting, we actually log into their accounts and look at their data to see what's been happening.

In many cases, clients have a history with various programmatic platforms. We've seen some situations where massive spend was going into certain websites without the client's understanding. Companies like DoubleVerify exist to police where ads are being served, but it's still disconcerting that so many companies are burning their ad budgets on ads that are never even seen.

There are already tech hurdles and manpower associated with running programmatic technology and creative. But programmatic ad buys often come with additional costs and fees, both transparent and hidden. And while some drawbacks can be alleviated by going through a third party display network, which buys ad inventory from pretty much the same place, it's still risky.

To reiterate, we do believe that programmatic display has a place. Particularly if your company can commit budgets of several million toward digital display advertising per year, and if you've already reached the opportunity ceiling on Facebook and Instagram: in that case, programmatic might be the right strategy for you. Leveraging the data and reach capabilities of programmatic can be a powerful strategy for brands of a certain size and with certain objectives.

Buying programmatically directly as a brand is the most transparent and clear cut way to do it. This would mean going direct to the Trade Desk or Doubleclick Bid Manager and seeing the platform fees transparently.

The next best alternative is to work with an honest and transparent agency who will buy on your behalf, will show you the rates they're being charged directly, and who will transparently show you what they're charging you. That fee may be 20% of media spend (on top of 16%+ platform fees), but it's far less than the often 50%+ markup that is applied to CPMs by the Big 5 and managed service programmatic partners (Steelhouse, Criteo).

What's more, the real power of programmatic goes beyond automating. Programmatic uses big data to profile existing customers across the web based on existing customer data. For Facebook specifically, programmatic plays at a different part of the funnel, but from a remarketing standpoint, it can be effective.

But in our experience auditing and working with hundreds of ecommerce brands of all sizes, Facebook and Adwords outperform programmatic the vast majority of the time. Before spending too much time or money evaluating your programmatic display opportunities, it's smarter to focus on achieving excellence on Facebook and Adwords first.

If you're already leaning on programmatic advertising, here are a few questions you might ask yourself to gauge the transparency of your technology vendor relationship:

- Do you know exactly where your media investments are made?

- Do you know what percentage of your media buy goes to third-party fees?

- Do you understand the daily management of your programmatic spend with agencies?

- Do you have a complex programmatic contract that makes hidden costs or fees hard to detect?

- Do you have multiple middlemen and layers between inventory source and buyer?

- Do you trust the quality of your ad inventory and placements?

One colleague of ours put it best:

"Letting managed service partners own reporting from their proprietary tracking platform's data is like letting people grade their own homework. They're going to give themselves a high grade. We recommend always having a 3rd party tracking and attribution platform in place, i.e., DoubleClick Campaign Manager. Meanwhile, always be skeptical of any network that says they can not serve through a 3rd party platform."

A word to the wise: When you lose transparency, you lose all control to optimize.

IS YOUR AGENCY ETHICALLY OUTSOURCING, OR INTENTIONALLY MISLEADING?

If your marketing agency is outsourcing, it's not necessarily an indication of badvertising.

If the workflow is transparent and the end performance is strong, most clients won't object, especially for a lower agency fee.

If we can deliver the same amount of work with cheaper labor, it's not always ad fraud or badvertising.

Some of the big agencies, for example, know they're not good at a given channel. This isn't an inherently evil practice, as long as it's not opaque to the end client.

What *is* fraud, however, is pretending: an agency developing an entire pitch and strategy around claiming head-to-tail ownership of the work.

You'll get bad value because you contracted this agency to do, say, six things; they do one, then subcontract the other five and mark it up with their own fee. And so you're not paying for what you thought you were.

One story comes to mind. A major, well known creative agency pitched a large brand on an AOR-style service that included performance marketing. The agency did not have the capability in-house and brought in a specialized performance marketing agency as a white-label partner to build and manage the majority of the performance marketing business for the client.

The first year was a massive success, as was the second year. But by that time, the creative agency desired to cut costs and hire their own team in-house to shore up profitability for the agency as a whole.

It's easy to predict what happened next. Quality of service dropped and within a year the client put out an RFP for a legitimate performance marketing agency. The creative agency has since dissolved their entire in-house performance marketing team.

Who lost here? Certainly the client did, but also the team that the creative agency hired to try to build this capability in-house, as well as the creative agency themselves, and the white labeled performance marketing agency. The reason why? Because the white-labeling was not transparent, and the creative agency was reaching to do something that was not in their DNA.

This is merely one of many stories. Why do we know about this? Because time and again, we have been the company that the big agency turns to when it realizes it has sold performance marketing and doesn't know how to execute. Including the agency mentioned above. It all goes back to transparency. Nobody should be taking credit for something they didn't do.

HOW IS YOUR AGENCY OPENING DOORS TO BUILD A FOUNDATION OF TRUST?

Perhaps the most egregious example of badvertising is when agencies or ad tech vendors prohibit clients from ownership and access to their accounts, and the reporting thereof.

In terms of ownership and access, any marketing agency, or any business for that matter, should be willing and happy to report on the work they're doing, and that reporting should be appropriately detailed to break down the results for each of the projects they're running.

Everything in a client relationship builds off a foundational exchange of trust. If an agency builds that into the relationship from day one, the project will start on a firm foundation of transparency. But if trust is broken, it's very hard to win it back.

One marketing director from an ecommerce company once told us that they had no idea how poorly their Facebook advertising accounts had been run until they were granted access. When they finally logged in, they learned that the account was not only tracking the wrong events, but their marketing agency also hadn't made a Facebook custom audience in twelve months. That's when the brand knew they had been taken advantage of for years.

This is not okay. We see far too many agencies who won't even give their clients access to their Facebook or Adwords accounts. Retaining clients by putting up walls and hiding what you're doing is questionable if not completely short-sighted.

The most common pattern we see is when agencies run campaigns from their own business Facebook page or Adwords account. This is to the agency's advantage, because once the client leaves, they'll have no future access to that data. This could be two years of valuable data that can't be transferred.

Often clients don't even know how to ask for access. The number of companies that enter into engagements where they don't have access to the data continues to shock us. We believe it must be an issue of education. Clients simply don't know to ask.

Encouraging clients to ask for access is just one more step toward true transparency and data ownership.

And it reaches beyond access to paid social accounts. This is about any type of reporting mechanism between vendor and client in a service relationship. We believe brands should not only have access to, but own their accounts.

What's your policy on access and ownership for your clients? Are you cagey about turning over assets, data, and other information to clients, or are you willing to open doors to build a foundation of trust in the relationship?

When it comes to transparency between clients and vendors, it's not only about what's being done, but what's not being done.

◆ ◆ ◆

The Association of National Advertisers (ANA) recently released another report entitled *Media Transparency: Prescriptions, Principles, and Processes for Marketers*. This report includes an updated media agency contract template with new provisions and revised definitions intended to increase transparency between clients and agencies.

According to their CEO Bob Liodice:

"While significant progress has been made in bringing more transparency to the relationships between advertisers and media buying agencies, much more is needed."

Preach on, Bob. There are several key points in ANA's report that you should be aware of, regardless of your role in the advertising industry:

- Advertisers should ensure that their contracts with media agencies include robust language to deliver full transparency.

- Advertisers should insist on robust and far-reaching audit rights, including tracking contract compliance and measuring the media value delivered.
- Advertisers must implement disciplined internal processes to deliver contracts designed to ensure strict accountability, rigorous process governance, and senior management oversight.

The verdict is in. In the digital marketing space, elevating trust and restoring confidence in the client-agency partnership has become paramount.

One last point on transaction data. The ANA notes that new language was added to their template to ensure advertisers have access to that data, and that their access or ability to leverage it isn't limited.

Here's the actual text from the Master Media Buying Services Agreement Template:

"Addition of defined term 'Transaction Data' (Sections 1.95, 6.17-6.18): Language was added to the template to ensure that advertisers have access to transaction data over which any vendor or media owner claims rights that limit an advertiser's access and/or ability to leverage transaction data. If access is denied by any supply chain participant, the agency should assist to remediate the issue and/or the advertiser may consider removing the vendor or media owner from future media purchases to ensure advertiser's unfettered access and control of transaction data critical to measurement and ROI."

The reckoning isn't coming, it's here.

We're thrilled that ANA is taking both an accountable and optimistic position with this addendum. Agencies will now be held more accountable on the side of communicating everything to marketers. And hopefully badvertising will be a thing of the past.

It's yet another step forward in creating a rising tide that lifts all boats in the digital marketing industry.

WHAT'S THE CASE FOR TRANSPARENCY FROM THE AGENCY'S PERSPECTIVE?

Truth in advertising has never been more relevant to agencies, nor to their clients.

This is particularly true in the retail space. Whether you're an agency, vendor, entrepreneur, or freelancer, if you want to build long term value, you should be radically transparent with your clients.

We've found that in long run, this approach actually nets higher-quality, more sustainable client relationships. If modern marketing firms want to stand out as the top service provider of choice, we highly recommend differentiating on the value proposition nobody expects: the truth.

Why?

The philosophical and altruistic response to that is because it's better for all of us as an industry. That's the spirit of Interactive Advertising Bureau (IAB), which is a standardized set of mutual protections for people that are doing business in this space because there wasn't one before. IAB creates guidelines for transparency.

Now as an individual agency, why would you be incentivized to, for example, not allow clients to own their ad accounts? On the surface, it's probably a little bit harder to answer that for people beyond "just be a good person," because financially, curtailing access does benefit an agency in the short term.

But in the great digital marketing rapture, you don't want to be on the wrong side of history. You don't want to be the guys who get left behind because you've been bad actors.

Agencies like us are out there looking for clients who are falling victim. And this book is geared toward making sure clients can identify when it's happening to them.

We would be remiss if we didn't conclude this section with general recommendations for agencies and companies to move towards more transparent and performance-oriented relationships.

Although this book's theme is primarily the agency-client relationship, the client-consumer relationship is worth referencing to extend our transparency philosophy. Recent advertising scandals are forcing brands to realize and reckon with the issue of data-sharing. Cambridge Analytica most notably gained access to 50 million Facebook users, if you recall. And let's not forget the data breach story with Experian, one of the largest credit agency data brokers in the world, whose 15 million customers had their private information exposed. These are just two bad actors giving digital marketing a bad name, but they have triggered fear in the hearts of consumers.

Many people don't trust Facebook and don't view the platform favorably. They feel it violates their privacy. The same goes for Google, albeit probably to a lesser extent. However, the general consumer does not seem to have made that connection and extended that point of view to Instagram. Yet.

People get freaked out by of data breaches and because they don't trust corporations with their data. *Oh wow, big companies are finding more ways to screw me over.* And that makes it harder for agencies like us to like do a good job.

The topic of consumer transparency merits its own book, so we'll stop there for now.

Point being, it's another reason agencies should communicate data transparency every step of the way.

Too many agencies have client dashboards that are hidden or obfuscated. They make sure clients see only the data stories that they want them to see. They prefer to preserve a tidy client narrative that only shows upsides.

Are you receiving real-time, transparent reporting from your agency? Do you get updates, iterations, and other project milestones that are accessible and expedient?

If not, it sounds like another episode of badvertising.

PART 4: THE FUTURE

"You don't need to make an entire organizational transformation to fight back against badvertising. You just have to start with a little bit of humility.

-**Ryan Markman**

WHERE DO WE GO NEXT?

Harvard Business Review recently published a particularly compelling article about marketing careers. Whitler and Morgan explore research that shows that CMOs have the lowest tenure of any role in the C-suite, averaging only 4.1 years.

Much of that has to do with the shift of what marketing used to be, versus where it is today. And what it used to be was less measurable.

But today and in the future, we can measure performance for a wide variety of channels and strategies, and that measurability will only continue to increase. There's a redefining of what the CMO's role is, and it holds agency people and other marketers accountable to real results.

And that's a good thing. Since measuring has become the norm, there will be less room for smoke and mirrors. Less room for badvertising. And more room for transparency.

One of the purposes behind this book is to help companies take back control. Whether they're with an agency that they're not comfortable with, or protecting themselves going forward.

And look, we understand. It's a little harder to be nimble and adapt on the cutting edge when you have an entire organization to worry about. Most people in marketing leadership positions are not going to be digital experts. Even if they have thirty years of experience and even if they have helped build a brand, that doesn't equate to an understanding of paid social tactics like shared post IDs and custom audiences.

Companies should always make sure they put people in key leadership positions who understand this world, to hold the agencies accountable and help companies understand how digital marketing services fit with the rest of the marketing plan.

The good news is, you don't need to make an entire organizational transformation to start fighting back against badvertising.

You just have to start with a little bit of humility.

It's hard for any agency to tactfully get across the level of opportunity in digital marketing for a big brand who's been taken advantage of (without making somebody look bad).

But it's not their fault. If someone doesn't have a lot of expertise and they thought they had a trusted agency partner, don't shoot the messenger, right?

Ultimately, we believe that we're not alone in our desire to create greater clarity and trust; to establish higher standards of accountability for digital brands; and to promote transparent business practices in the digital marketing world.

As for the many players in the digital marketing ecosystem, here's what we believe the future could be.

Small brands will confidently invest in digital marketing to create growth revenue for their startups.

Enterprise brands will turn marketing into a profit center and create the highest leverage for their brands.

Agencies and tech companies will retain their employees and clients, differentiating their firms through transparent service.

Investors will proactively hold their brands accountable through the objectivity and data driven results of performance marketing.

Join us in putting an end to badvertising.

Take back control.

Because we're tired of losing sleep over marketing done poorly.

APPENDIX

PREPARING YOUR BRAND FOR GROWTH

Digital marketing agencies are becoming a commodity.

There are 15,000+ to choose from, and it can be tough to discern the experts from the scams.

This is also a common cause for the recent trend toward taking marketing in-house. In this final bonus section, we're going to help you get your brand into the best shape to make the right choice for your marketing objectives.

Let's start with a common misconception:

"If our company just advertised more, we'd get more business."

Not necessarily.

Depending on what type of company you are, it may be the wrong time to get serious about paid media. If your goal is positive ROI on paid advertising, there are several critical elements you need to figure out about your company before you start running ads in a meaningful way (i.e. $3,000+ per month).

For example, if your beautiful ecommerce website just went live yesterday, but you don't have tracking infrastructure in place, then it's not the time to spend $5,000/month on paid ads. The complete lack of feedback means not measuring ad spend correct and will be like lighting your investment on fire.

Now, if your brand still needs to get its digital house in order, to put your business into the best possible shape for launching your digital marketing effort, that's no problem. Before you spend a dime on paid advertising with an agency, we want to make sure that you're in the best possible position capitalize on that effort first.

Next we're going to give you further context about structuring your digital marketing strategy to maximize conversions, but also help you spot and fix any leaks in your current tactics. Through these lists, you will be challenged to consider many elements of marketing that you may not have thought of yet, along with the relative importance of each.

Our categories will be as follows: Devices, Polish, Product, Usability, Conversion, Focus, Traction, Financial, and Tracking. Pencils ready!

DEVICES:

We know, it's been the year of mobile for a decade. But that doesn't make it any less true. If your site is not optimized to be viewed in somebody's hand while they're walking down the street, you aren't ready for paid. Ask yourself this:

- Is your site mobile responsive?

- Are there any load time issues?

POLISH:

Companies tend to underestimate the impact that small things have. As a growing audience repeatedly visits your site, sloppy mistakes will multiply into revenue lost. Don't burn your ad budget until you consider:

- Do you have any broken links?
- Do you have missing images?
- Are there any typos?

PRODUCT:

A huge hurdle in ecommerce is that customers would rather see and touch something in person before buying. Here are potential issues worth discussing with your team:

- Do you have high-quality images?
- Are your photos sized correctly?
- Do you have interactive zoom features to mimic tactile sensation?
- Have you featured reviews for products?

USABILITY:

The only thing more frustrating than a site that takes forever to load, is a fast-loading site that doesn't reflect user expectations. Before spending any money on paid ads, answer these questions:

- Is your site speed up to par? (Test it now with Google PageSpeed Insights.)
- Is the site behaving the way customers expect it to?

CONVERSION:

By setting up your website to encourage conversion-positive actions (anything from viewing a product page to signing up for an email list), each and every paid site visit that you generate becomes more valuable. Consider these questions before moving forward with your paid efforts:

- Are you capturing permission assets like email addresses?

- Is your site catching ancillary conversions, i.e. positive actions that don't involve purchase?

- Are product pages easy to find and interact with?

- Will your shopper find sufficient motivation to make a purchase on your site? (Motivating factors include descriptive text, clear and appetizing images, and discount codes.)

- What sources of friction (high prices, broken links, insufficient product images, awkward checkout flow) might prevent the shopper from making a purchase?

FOCUS:

Your website needs to speak the customer's language, tap into their belief system, and reinforce your overarching campaign narrative. From the headline to the copy, everything should link back to the north star of your brand. Ask this:

- Does your headline speak directly to customer needs?
- Are you creating value in the highest-impact areas of the site?
- Are you speaking to customers, or just describing products?

TRACTION:

An established ecommerce brand is going to take to paid media a lot more quickly and effectively than one that doesn't already have organic traction. Large companies can use many conversion events from existing traffic, build accurate look alike audiences, and so on. Ask:

- What is your existing organic engagement?
- Is there existing love you can amplify?

FINANCIAL:

Before you start breaking the bank on paid advertising, let's explore your current ad spend. This gives us a sense of where you're at and where you're going. Think about a few more questions:

- How much are you already spending on paid?
- What revenue bucket do you fall into?

Even if you have made very few sales, it doesn't necessarily mean you should try paid ads. However, expect that your ads won't convert well off the bat. Paid can be a solid way for you to learn how customers respond to your site and products.

TRACKING:

We wouldn't be a performance marketing company without mentioning this last one. If you aren't accurately measuring your current performance, future performance will suffer. Without consistent naming conventions, it's hard to tell what's working and what's not. Make sure you score your site on these final questions:

- Do you have an effective tracking infrastructure in place?
- Is your Facebook Pixel set up?
- Are your Google Analytics accounts set up?
- Is your conversion tracking set up?
- Do you have ecommerce tracking enabled?

If your company successfully answered these questions, then you are ready to hire an agency to set up your paid campaigns and begin converting traffic into revenue. But if you didn't have as many answers as you were hoping for, now you have a chance to fix any leaks to prepare your brand to maximize conversions in the future.

ABOUT THE AUTHORS

Kevin Simonson, CEO/Co-Founder

Kevin has probably influenced your online behavior. He has worked with hundreds of companies, from Bonobos to Carnival Cruise Lines, spending over $100 million in digital advertising to convince people to take various actions online. He has lectured at Harvard and General Assembly and is an advisor to several companies on social advertising

John Pellinghelli, Co-Founder

John is an expert in all things digital advertising and analytics. John specializes in retail and B2B lead gen with experience driving efficient growth at scale for Fortune 1000 companies like Nike, ADP, Under Armour and VC/PE backed firms such as Mack Weldon, Bonobos, and Canada Goose.

Ryan Markman, COO

As COO of Metric Digital, Ryan leads strategy, sales, and finance. Previously, Ryan served as GM of Y Combinator-backed adtech platform Boostable. Ryan also advised Private Equity and Fortune 1000 clients at Bain & Company

ABOUT METRIC DIGITAL

Metric Digital is a modern performance marketing agency that specializes in ecommerce. We're obsessed with driving high ROI growth for our clients. We use Paid Search, Paid Social, Email Marketing, and SEO to drive revenue and accomplish measurable goals for brands of all sizes.

Our firm powers marketing for the best, most disruptive D2C brands. In the past several years, Metric Digital has helped companies drive sustainable growth that helped fuel their acquisitions, IPOs, or next funding rounds, such as Canada Goose (IPO), Bonobos (Acquired), Hired.com (Series C). Also, many of our clients are on the IAB 250 list, including JackThreads, Mack Weldon, Hint Water, and Nature Box.

To read case studies from some our clients, visit us online at **www.metricdigital.com**

Made in the USA
Middletown, DE
17 January 2019